FOR MY MOM AND DAD.
(I DID IT!)

WOMEN HEROES DEPICTED IN THE BOOK

Front endpapers (by row, front to back, left to right): Toni Morrison; Maggie Nichols; Alexandria Ocasio-Cortez; Simone Biles; Mari Copeny; Ava DuVernay; Wangari Maathai; Marlee Matlin; Sylvia Rivera; Shirley Chisholm; Bernadette Devlin; Wilma Rudolph; Claudette Colvin; Rosalind Franklin; Hedy Lamarr; Frida Kahlo; Amelia Earhart; Zora Neale Hurston; Josephine Baker; Lillian Leitzel; Jeannette Rankin; Clara Lemlich; Nellie Bly; Sojourner Truth; Ching Shih

Pages 16–17 (from right front to back left): Tarana Burke; Malala Yousafzai; Ada Lovelace; Eliza Suggs; Ida B. Wells; Alice de Rivera; Huda Sha'arawi; Marsha P. Johnson; Judy Heumann; Lady Murasaki; Artemisia Gentileschi; Susan La Flesche Picotte; Queen Emma of Hawai'i; FloJo; Patsy Mink; Bessie Coleman; Lucy Stone; Harriet Tubman; Angela Davis; Gladys Bentley; Christine Jorgensen; Sarojini Naidu; Mary Wollstonecraft; Ruby Bridges; Sappho; Edmonia Lewis; Victoria Woodhull; Mourning Dove; Christine de Pizan; Constance Lytton; Annette Kellermann; Chipeta (White Singing Bird); Chien-Shiung Wu; Boudicca; Coretta Scott King

Back endpapers (by row, front to back, left to right): Anaiah Thomas; Greta Thunberg; Sudha Chandran; Rachael Denhollander; Meryl Davis; Serena Williams; Cheryl Marie Wade; Geraldine Ferraro; Sandra Day O'Connor; Shirley Ann Jackson; Coccinelle (Jacqueline Charlotte Dufresnoy); Rosa Parks; Sister Rosetta Tharpe; Marian Anderson; Fanny Brice; Aida Overton Walker; Jane Addams; Annie Jones; Elizabeth Garrett Anderson; Sarah Winnemucca; Olympe de Gouges; Ann Radcliffe; Toypurina; Gráinne Mhaol; Trotula of Salerno

[Imprint]
MAKE YOUR MARK

A part of Macmillan Publishing Group, LLC
120 Broadway, New York, NY 10271

About This Book
The art for this book was drawn in pencil and colored digitally in Clip Studio Paint. The text was set in Rockwell and Filosofia, and the display type is Filosofia. The book was edited by Erin Stein and designed by Jessica Lauren Chung. The production was supervised by Jie Yang, and the production editor was Ilana Worrell.

Library of Congress Cataloging-in-Publication Data is available.
ISBN 978-1-250-77450-7 (hardcover)

Our books may be purchased in bulk for promotional, educational, or business use. Please contact your local bookseller or the Macmillan Corporate and Premium Sales Department at (800) 221-7945 ext. 5442 or by email at MacmillanSpecialMarkets@macmillan.com.

Imprint logo designed by Amanda Spielman
First edition, 2021
1 3 5 7 9 10 8 6 4 2
mackids.com

This book's author sincerely enjoys
A nefarious lady who always employs
Cunning wit and nerve and frightful daring.
But if you steal this book, you'll be left despairing.

ROSIE
THE RIVETER

THE LEGACY OF AN AMERICAN ICON

SARAH DVOJACK

{Imprint}
MAKE YOUR MARK

NEW YORK

Rosie the Riveter was born all grown up in 1942.

It was the middle of the Second World War, and everybody
needed her because everything was coming apart.

Rosie was a riveter, after all.

Riveting is a way to hold pieces
together to make something
strong and powerful.
Like overalls or a ship or a bridge
or maybe even a world.

Women weren't allowed to fight in the war, but they were capable of doing all the other jobs that needed doing.

Some of those jobs, like riveting ships and airplanes and bridges, were usually done by men. But the men were mostly gone, busy taking the rivets out of the world.

That's how Rosie was born all grown-up in 1942.

She came out of a song that shared her name,
and people saw her strong arms on a poster.

She took a lunch break on a magazine cover,
and starred in a movie, too.

But parts of Rosie existed a long time before movies and magazines and posters.

Parts of her had always existed. Parts of her always will.

Rosies couldn't fight in wars back then,
but their strong arms fought for room in the
workplace, every workplace, when the
war was over and the men came home.

People pushed them this way and that way,
whether or not they chose that way or this,
but Rosies pushed back. And so more
women pushed back, too.

Women had rallied many times before, but Rosie gave them a symbol to use in their fight. She was a celebrity and a friendly face, and she didn't scare people. She also couldn't be thrown in prison or shamed into going home.

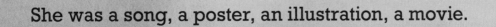

She was a song, a poster, an illustration, a movie.

And then she was a movement.

Her strong arms held open doors long enough for women to stick their hands and arms and shoulders and bodies through and throw the doors open wider. And when the doors threatened to fall shut, Rosie held on. But there were so many others behind her now, and their hands, and arms, and shoulders, and bodies— and voices—kept marching through.

People know her by her polka-dot red bandanna and rolled-up sleeves, but she wears other uniforms, too.

Rosie the Riveter is not just one woman.

She is every woman.

Even if your name isn't Rosie.

Even if you're not a riveter.

Even if you're still just a kid.

And Rosie isn't just a riveter.

She's a welder.

A teacher.

An athlete.

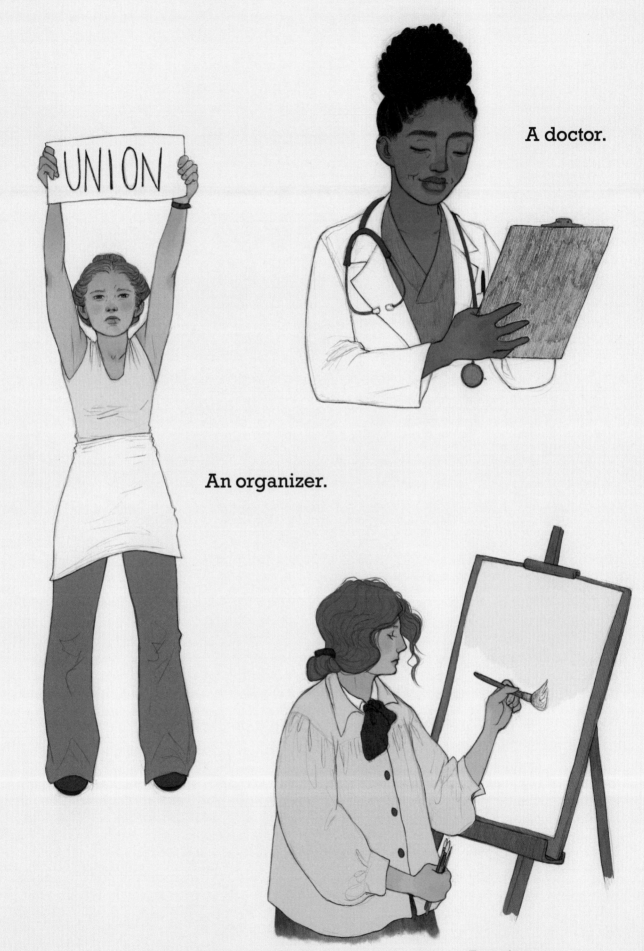

UNION

An organizer.

A doctor.

A painter.

A friend.

She persists and perseveres. She endures.

Rosie the Riveter is more grown up than ever, but she does not grow old. She reminds us what is possible and how much work it took to come this far, how much work we still have to do.

She reminds us that she—and therefore we—are able, and capable, and *real*.

Generations have followed her and used her image, used her power, used her strength.

Like a rivet.

LEARN MORE ABOUT
ROSIE THE RIVETER

WOMEN, WORK, AND WAR

These days, it's not unusual or surprising for the women in our lives to financially support themselves or their families. Whether they have one job or three, work from home or travel across the world for business, women (trans and cis) can be seen at work! We see them in factories and courtrooms, grocery stores and schools. Today we know that women can do any job and do it well.

But this was not always the case. For a long time, women in countries like the United States, where Rosie was popular, were only expected to do certain kinds of jobs, if any. Many societies think a woman's role is at home, raising children and running the household. This is a great and difficult job itself, but women now have the *choice* to do other kinds of work, too. Each woman has her own goals and ideas of what she would like to do in her lifetime.

A woman's economic class and race, and the combination of the two, dictated what was acceptable and what was not. This has improved in some ways, but is still true for many women in the United States and around the world. Even if they could get hired, women were paid less than men for the same work, and non-white women were paid less than white women. While there has been improvement, this is still true today.

In 2018, women earned an average of eighty-five cents compared to every dollar that a man made in the same job. That means it would take roughly forty extra days of work for a woman to earn the same pay as a man!

By the end of the Industrial

Revolution, which took place between 1760 and 1840, women were generally not encouraged or even allowed to go to colleges or universities to continue their education, keeping them away from jobs as doctors, lawyers, and scientists, for example. And though women were hired as teachers, they were expected to quit their jobs if they started a family.

Societal reforms and protests were leading a change by the time World War I began in 1914. Women's suffrage, which is the right to vote, as well as the rise of general strikes and organized labor, were pushing society toward progress, inch by inch. Women were going to college at a higher rate and slowly entering a wider array of fields. But many people still thought they were not supposed to be there. And college was often seen as a way for a woman to meet a husband, not to get a job. And for non-white women, even this option was limited.

But then World War I changed everything. This was the first modern "total war." A total war requires all the resources from the countries involved to go toward war efforts. Men were conscripted into armies across the world, which required women to take the jobs left behind. There were far fewer men around to do them!

Many died in the war and many more Americans died during the flu pandemic of 1918. More women joined the workforce out of necessity. Their country needed them. Then, in 1929, the stock market crashed and the Great Depression began. Jobs became scarce and didn't pay very much. To make matters even worse, a severe drought caused dust storms that covered farms and prairies in mountains of dirt, killing livestock and crops and forcing farming families to leave their homes behind. *Everyone* in a family had to work if they could find a job.

By the 1940s, it was more acceptable in America for women to work as clerks or secretaries. But those weren't the jobs that needed to be filled when World War II began. This was another total war. As during World War I, women were needed in industrial labor, to make ammunition and airplanes, to work alongside men who couldn't go to war; and non-white women's hands were needed, too. But many women still stayed at home, or were told to stay at home by family. And yet, they were needed elsewhere. Rosie became the tool to get women to work.

The Rosie the Riveter campaign was created by employers in (mainly) manufacturing and industrial jobs. They needed to get all women, even reluctant ones, into what had traditionally been men's jobs. Rosie stressed the patriotic importance of going into the workforce during the war. No one else could do these essential jobs, but Rosies could! By 1943, over three hundred thousand women worked in the aircraft industry, making up 65 percent of the industry's labor force, compared to 1 percent during the pre-war years.

While this campaign urged women into these wartime jobs, it was with the expectation that they would return home once the war was over. And, for the most part, this ended up being true. When the men came home, women were demoted or fired from many industrial jobs.

But WWII had dramatically changed the world. A fuse had been lit, and Rosie was one of those sparks. Over the decades that followed, people fought for rights across many disenfranchised groups, and Rosie evolved from a wartime image with a very specific purpose to become a symbol of the feminist movement; the right for all women to work where they want, doing what they want, for equal pay; and the right to choose the path they want. Just put on that polka-dot scarf and people think of strength and a fighting spirit.

WAS ROSIE A REAL PERSON?

Over the decades, several different real-life women have been put forth as the inspiration for Rosie, but the truth is hard to know for sure! *Many* real women inspired, or *may* have inspired, different images of Rosie throughout WWII. There were also other types of Rosies, such as Wanda the Welder.

Whichever women had their hands (or scarves) in inspiring Rosie, what we *can* say is that the term came from the song.

THE SONG

Written by Redd Evans and John Jacob Loeb in 1943, "Rosie the Riveter" was a huge hit in the United States and is the origin for the name. But was there an origin for the origin?

The idea for the song (and possibly Rosie's name) was allegedly inspired by Rosalind P. Walter, who worked the night shift building the F4U Corsair fighter plane.

The choice of the name "Rosie" might also have come from Rosina "Rosie" Bonavita, who worked for Convair in San Diego, California.

Another potential inspiration for the concept of a Rosie was Veronica Foster, Canada's poster girl in 1941 (aka Ronnie, the Bren Gun Girl).

Later, after the song was written, many credited the inspiration to Rose Will Monroe, who was a riveter at the Willow Run aircraft factory in Ypsilanti, Michigan, building B-24 bombers. She starred in a promotional film about the war effort during the time the song was popular.

THE WESTINGHOUSE POSTER

Though this beloved illustration by J. Howard Miller is now the most well-known Rosie the Riveter image, it was originally only displayed for Westinghouse employees for about two weeks in February 1943.

Westinghouse is an electric and manufacturing company that still exists today. During WWII, after making equipment like radars for jet planes, and ground-based airport lighting, they were offered a contract with the United States to produce plastic helmet liners. The colorful "We Can Do It!" tagline probably helped boost morale as everyone worked overtime to get things done for the war effort.

At no point during the war, and indeed not until the 1980s, was the woman in the poster even called Rosie! (Though it's very clear that she was inspired by the same working women who inspired Rosie.)

Naomi Parker Fraley might have been the visual reference for Miller's illustration. Photos of her sporting a polka-dot scarf were released by United Press International before the poster was created, so the artist could have seen the photographs in the news. For a long time, Naomi Parker Fraley was misidentified as Geraldine Doyle (then Hoff) of Michigan, another "Rosie."

THE ROCKWELL ILLUSTRATION

Norman Rockwell's *Saturday Evening Post* cover was published on May 29, 1943. We know he was deliberately using the Rosie the Riveter character—look at her name on the lunch box!

Rockwell's model for this session was Mary Doyle Keefe (no relation to Geraldine Doyle), a nineteen-year-old telephone operator. Though she wasn't as muscular as Rockwell's Rosie, she *was* holding a sandwich when she sat for reference photos! Rockwell chose a pose based on a well-known painting by Michelangelo, which made his Rosie even more popular.

Rockwell's illustration was a huge hit at the time, and the original painting sold for $5 million in 2002! Mary Doyle Keefe received $10 for her modeling—that's about $150 today.

THE MOVIE

Released in 1944 and directed by Joseph Santley, the movie stars Jane Frazee as Rosalind "Rosie" Warren, who works at a defense plant in California (much like some of the real-life Rosie inspirations mentioned earlier). The movie is a lighthearted comedy with a little bit of romance, involving two men who also work at the plant. It didn't do much to add to the Rosie mythology, but during WWII, it was common to make lighthearted features to show to the soldiers, and to entertain their families back home.